Three Short Plays

by

Anne Le Marquand Hartigan

ϙϸ

CHISWICK BOOKS

LONDON

www.chiswickbooks.com

First published in 2016 by Chiswick Books
2 Prebend Gardens, Chiswick, London W4 1TW
email: info@chiswickbooks.com
website: www.chiswickbooks.com

In Other Worlds copyright © Anne Le Marquand Hartigan 2003, Strings copyright © Anne Le Marquand Hartigan 1981, Cake copyright © Anne Le Marquand Hartigan 1984.

Anne Le Marquand Hartigan is hereby identified as author of these plays in accordance with section 77 of the Copyright, Designs and Patents Act 1988. The author has asserted her moral rights.

All rights whatsoever in these plays are strictly reserved and application for performance etc. should be made before commencement of rehearsal to email: rights@annehartigan.com. No performance may be given unless a licence has been obtained, and no alterations may be made in the title or the text of the play without the author's prior written consent. This book is sold subject to the condition that it shall not by way of trade or otherwise be circulated without the publisher's consent in any form of binding or cover or circulated electronically other than that in which it is published and without a similar condition including this condition being imposed on any subsequent purchaser.

This is a work of fiction. Names, characters, places and incidents either are products of the author's imagination or are used fictitiously. Any resemblance to actual events or locales or persons, living or dead, is entirely coincidental.

British Library Cataloguing in Publication Data. A catalogue record for this book is available from the British Library.
ISBN: 978-0-9928692-9-8

Cover image from a painting by Anne Le Marquand Hartigan.

Also by the author

Plays

Beds, *Chiswick Books, 2016*
I Do Like To Be Beside The Seaside, *Chiswick Books, 2016*
Jersey Lilies, *Chiswick Books, 2016*
La Corbière, *Chiswick Books, 2016*
The Secret Game, *Chiswick Books, 2014*

Poetry

Unsweet Dreams, *Salmon Poetry, 2011*
To Keep The Light Burning, *Salmon Poetry, 2008*
Nourishment, *Salmon Poetry, 2005*
Immortal Sins, *Salmon Poetry, 1995*
Now is a Moveable Feast, *Salmon Poetry, 1991*
Return Single, *Beaver Row Press, 1986*
Long Tongue, *Beaver Row Press, 1982*

Prose

Clearing the Space, *Salmon Poetry, 1996*

To my grandchildren, Diarmuid, Florence, Colm, Elizabeth, Inis, Patrick, Zoë, Cherri, Naoise, Ruaidhrí, Euan, Freya, Guaire, Sadhbh, Iona, Dominic, Rosanna and Taig and my granddaughter-in-law, Andrea.

Contents

In Other Worlds   7

Strings   41

Cake   71

In Other Worlds

A play in one act

First production

In Other Worlds was commissioned and first produced in 2003 by Ohio Northern University with the following cast:

MAGGIE BYRNE	Kilee Hill
MIKE BYRNE	David Garwood
SARAH BYRNE/NURSE TWO	Katy O'Leary
WOMAN/NURSE ONE	Eileen Earnest
Director	Rita Henderson

Characters

MAGGIE BYRNE *wife and mother, early fifties*

MIKE BYRNE *husband and father, early fifties*

SARAH BYRNE *daughter, a bright, smart woman in her mid-to-late twenties also plays NURSE TWO*

THE WOMAN *unknown, unnamed and mysterious. She is elegant in a black suit, red satin blouse and high heels, also plays NURSEONE*

NURSE ONE

NURSE TWO

Set

A present day intensive care unit in a hospital. It is simple, stark, cold and surreal. There is a machine with screens that monitors the heart, pulse, lungs etc. Tubes and wires are attached with pads to the patient. There is a drip and transfusion apparatus. None of this need be realistic, should be simple and surreal rather than naturalistic. One or two chairs. The whole is very bare, simple, strange, no clutter.

There are three places where the nurses' white coats can hang. Two white coats hang there. They should hang as if suspended in mid-air. There is an exit immediately upstage and to the right of these coats. Three pairs of rubber gloves hang on their own in the same way. Three pairs of angels' wings also hang in the same way.

The set is roughly in two parts: the bed and patient left of centre stage, outside the intensive care unit is right of centre stage, though this is not marked in any way. The actors define it as they move and talk.

Colour: steel, purple and white.

Sound

Intensive care unit sounds, ambulance sirens, internal body sounds, breathing, heartbeat, blood flow, etc. The sound of a dog barking. These sounds, unnaturally loud, are used as a kind of background music. When the mobile phone is used, especially at the beginning of the play, it needs to be louder than an ordinary phone to make sure all the audience hears it.

Note

The word 'craic' is the Irish word for fun. It is used frequently in Ireland. The expression 'great gas,' also means good fun, having a good time. This expression can also apply to a person, you can say: 'ah sure, he's great gas.'

Bringing the audience into the play from the very beginning by use of the mobile phone, and again when the wife comes back to talk to the audience, underlines that we too, all of us, inhabit many worlds that we are separated from, and connected to, at the same time. All the characters in the play, as we are ourselves, are in situations with each other and with other people who are outside the play - lovers, sons, dogs and so on. The intensive care unit is chilling with its instruments that enable us to survive. And because they are machines, they lack 'the milk of human kindness.' Our powerful modern technology (such as the mobile phone,) connects us closely and instantly yet sometimes, as in the case of the intensive care unit, it can frighten us.

Scene One

*The lights go down in the auditorium and on stage.
From the darkness a mobile phone is heard ringing from
MAGGIE BYRNE sitting as a member of the audience. This
must be loud and preferably a silly ringtone. MAGGIE
fumbles in her pocket for the phone which continues to
ring. She apologises to all around her. While answering the
phone she jumps up and scrambles through the audience.*

MAGGIE

> *Answering her mobile phone.*
>
> What?
>
> *Pause.*
>
> What did you say? Where? Oh my God!
>
> *Pause.*
>
> Is he in danger?
>
> *Pause.*
>
> What has happened? Say that again? Yes, Yes. I
> know the hospital. Oh yes, I will. Oh my God,
> yes thank you.
>
> I will. I will. He is alive? He is? Oh I'll get there,
> I'll get there... I will, oh I will, oh my God... I'm

coming at once... now...

During this she is moving through the audience and continues to do so, apologising to everyone.

Oh, I am so sorry, please forgive me - I am sorry but I just have had dreadful news. I have to get out. I'm so sorry. I really am. Please forgive me. Sorry. Sorry. It's an emergency, but oh, it's so...

The actor can ad-lib as she bumbles her way through the rows of people in the audience causing disruption. She can react as she thinks fit if members of the audience talk to her. She rushes to the exit. She exits. A sudden, short and complete silence.

In the darkness, sound of difficult breathing, unnaturally loud. Then loud and sudden ambulance siren. The sound of a heartbeat, loud.

Now the audience is disrupted by NURSE ONE entering and pushing a stretcher on wheels. MIKE BYRNE, lies on this. He is unconscious. NURSE TWO, played by the actor who plays SARAH, jumps up from the audience, pulls on her white coat and rushes to join the stretcher.

Together the two NURSES push the patient onto the stage where they set up MIKE in the unit, attaching him to various machines, transfusion, drip, etc. NURSES bare his chest to attach machines. MIKE is unconscious.

Sound changes from emergency sounds to machines of the unit etc. Various screens show the monitoring of MIKE's condition. The NURSES care for him efficiently and silently. The NURSES hover, help, protect, guard, are quiet, but are ineffective against death.

A spotlight on MIKE must indicate he is in another state. From the back of the auditorium MAGGIE enters swiftly down toward the stage while she is making a call on her mobile. She is trying to contact her son Billy but just gets his answer phone This action overlaps with the action on the stage.

NURSES

The NURSES drop these words through MAGGIE's phone call, they can be repeated.

Oxygen, transfusion, blood, pulse, temperature, saline, antibiotics, trauma.

Sounds of machines continue. NURSE TWO

leaves, hanging her white coat up and becomes SARAH. Exit.

MAGGIE

On her mobile phone.

Damn, damn, Same as always, just the bloody answer phone.

She proceeds to leave a message for her son.

Billy, Billy, listen. I've some awful news. I'm… I'm on my way to the hospital. I've just heard Dad's been taken ill. No, no, I mean he's had an accident… Your Dad, Billy. He's OK. I think… I mean I don't know what's happened. They told me they had to operate immediately and to come at once… Oh, please phone back at once and come, come, now! He's in Our Lady's Hospital. You know it. He's in Intensive Care. Oh I do need you, so please come. Don't ignore me… Not this time. Not now, Billy please. Listen… Oh, damn it's cut me off…

She rushes into the intensive care unit. NURSE ONE goes to meet and reassure her.

Oh, how is Mike? My husband. How is he? What… what happened?

Is he going to…? What's happening to him now?

Is he in pain?

They go to MIKE. MAGGIE sits by him. She speaks quickly, hardly waiting for the nurse's reply, interrupting her.

NURSE ONE

> He's holding his own at the moment. He has large internal injuries. To stop the bleeding the doctors had to operate immediately. He's lost a lot of blood, the poor man.

MAGGIE

> God help him. What happened to him? How did it happen?

NURSE ONE

> We are not sure. We have no details yet. They think it might have been a hit and run.

MAGGIE

> Hit and run? How can it be a hit and run... You mean he was hit on purpose?

NURSE ONE

> We don't know what happened to him but it seems that the car did not stop. His injuries conform with being hit by a travelling car. He is a strong man but he's lucky to be with us.

MAGGIE

> Oh. I don't understand. How is he? He looks so bad.

NURSE ONE

> He is holding his own, but you must know he is a fighter...

MAGGIE

> Oh, yes, he is a fighter alright. Can he hear me? If I speak to him?

NURSE ONE

> He may. Very likely he can. But he is unconscious so he is not suffering...

MAGGIE

> Not suffering? Oh, he looks like suffering. This is suffering - terrible, terrible, suffering. *Whispers.* Is he in danger? Might he die?
>
> *NURSE ONE bends close to MAGGIE. We do not hear NURSE ONE's answer. MAGGIE sits close to her husband. MIKE is unconscious and we hear his thoughts, in this dream-like state, on voice-over. In this speech he is concerned for his young dog who he loves. He whistles for his dog and instructs her as he is training her.*

Should sound as if in the open air as MIKE talks and plays with his dog. He whistles for his dog and calls her. He adopts different tones for each instruction as dog trainers do. His tone is also contented as he enjoys concentrating on training his dog.

MIKE

>Come, come, come here, girl. There's the girl. Sit there. You're the great girl altogether. Sit. Sit. Good dog. Lie down. Lie down. Good girl, good girl.

SARAH

>*She speaks on her mobile phone to her boyfriend, Brian.*
>
>Darling. It's me. Just leaving you a message, Brian, sweetheart. Horrible things happening, you've no idea... Can't believe it. I'm on my way to the hospital. My dad's done something dreadful to himself, God knows what. Mum's there already. Apparently it's bad. He's in Intensive. Trust him to be dramatic. God that sounds shit. Well, it is. Bloody shit. So I can't join you this afternoon, darling. Oh darling, please forgive me. Oh fuck it. Well, we will,

won't we? Later on? Please, please, please phone me! Phone now. Shit. I need you. Please phone, Brian, as soon as you get this message honey. OK? Bye.

Kisses into the phone. She dials again and gets her mother, MAGGIE.

Mum?

We see MAGGIE take out her mobile and move away from the bed and out of the intensive care unit as she listens to her daughter. SARAH leaves spaces for her mother's replies which we do not hear. However the pace is quick. NURSE ONE leaves and hangs up her coat.

SARAH

What's up? What's Dad up to? You can't speak to him? Dad can't talk? That's a new one. Yes, I'm on my way.

Pause.

Mum give over. Billy won't answer, don't kid yourself. You'll only give yourself grief. Yep, I'll be there soon. Take it easy. Dad will be OK. You know Dad - he's a survivor. Look, I'm driving so I must stop. See you soon. Yes, as quick as possible, OK? Bye.

SARAH switches off the phone. MAGGIE stands and remains outside the unit. THE WOMAN enters and stands close by MIKE. She is very self-contained, and assured. She has a still quality.

MIKE

On voice-over, he speaks to himself in his mind.
I feel cold, Why am I cold? Look here, couldn't you do something about it? I mean it's the least you could do, isn't it ? Give a man a bit of warmth? Come on now, I'm bloody freezing. Don't you feel it? My dog needs her dinner. Get her out of the cold and feed her won't you? Don't just stand there. She's only a young thing, she needs care. Her nuts are in a bag under the sink. I can hear her whining, she needs a meal. Then bring her here to me. I need her, she'll keep me warm.

Pause.

That's better. That's much better. All better now.

THE WOMAN leaves MIKE's side, exits the intensive care unit, and puts on a white coat to become NURSE ONE. She attends to MIKE and the machines. At the same time MAGGIE and

SARAH meet stage right outside the intensive care unit. They embrace and hold each other.

MAGGIE

> *Urgently. She has seen or thinks she has seen, THE WOMAN.*
>
> Who was that? That woman? Who was she?

SARAH

> What woman?

MAGGIE

> That woman in a dark suit. You saw her. She was there, next to the bed, close to Mike. Who was she?

SARAH

> There was nobody. I saw no one. There was no one - only nurses.

MAGGIE

> Don't treat me like a fool. I saw her. Tall, dark, good-looking. Never set eyes on her before - so who the hell was she?
>
> *NURSE ONE cares for MIKE, monitors the machines, etc.*

SARAH

> For God's sake Mum, cop yourself on. There's

just the staff here - do keep your voice down...

MAGGIE

> Look, my girl, only family are allowed in here. Jesus, Mary and Joseph, no one else can be in here - should be in here...

SARAH

> Mum, calm down. I know how difficult this is for you, for us. I didn't see anyone, but I expect if there was someone there, she was a doctor. They don't let anyone in.

MAGGIE

> Perhaps she wasn't just anyone. How do I know? Did Dad have anyone else? Mike talked to you. He didn't talk to me. Not for a long time. Not for ages...
>
> *Pause.*
>
> You know something. You do! You do! You're covering up...
>
> *NURSE ONE leaves and takes off her white coat and hangs it up. She stays out of the unit and stands still at the side of the action, out of the main lighting but there as a presence.*

SARAH

> Fuck's sake Mum, I've better things to do than cover for Dad. I'm covering nothing. Don't get paranoid. I haven't spoken to Dad either, not for... Oh not for ages, absolute ages...

MAGGIE

> Oh yes! Is that so? But you did. You did in the past. He adored you. The sun shone out of your little arse...

SARAH

> Well, that bit of sunshine ended with a bang...

MAGGIE

> And I'm not paranoid - don't talk like that. You could do no wrong as far as he was concerned. You just had to wiggle a little finger and he became putty in your hands. It was disgusting.

SARAH

> Mum, it's you that's being disgusting. Will you shut it, please? All that's so past. Dead in the past.

MAGGIE

> Well, if it is in the past it's because of that man. That fellow of yours. Brian, you and Brian.

SARAH

> Mum, leave Brian out of this...

MAGGIE

> What do you think it's like for me seeing you wasting yourself on a... on a... complete... bastard?

SARAH

> Mum. Cool it. Dad's ill. That's what matters now. There was no woman - see! You're just seeing things. If you can't get it together, I'm going. I just don't need this.

MAGGIE

> That's it, just walk away if anything is unpleasant. It's... obscene to see you with the husband of my best friend. A man with teenage children. You don't know what you've done to my life.
>
> *Pause.*
>
> *Very quietly, almost to herself:*
>
> I haven't a life any more...

SARAH

> Stop it Mother. Mum, just shut up and stop it. We've got to deal with now, with Dad.

MAGGIE

> I'm tired of minding Dad.

SARAH

> Well perhaps you won't have to much longer...

MAGGIE

> God! Don't say things like that. Things are bad enough as they are without you...

SARAH

> Mum, I can't and I won't, take this crap. Things are as they are. We just have to deal with them. Here. Now. We have no alternative.
>
> *Silence.*

MAGGIE

> Of course, you're right. I'm sorry, love. I'm sorry...
>
> I phoned Billy. Of course he didn't answer. I left a message.

SARAH

> Give it up, Mum. Forget my baby brother Billy. He won't put himself out for anything or anyone. Forget it, Mum. Let's just get on with the here and now. We've this to cope with. It's enough.

MAGGIE

> You see, where is my life? What have I got? Now Mike's like this.
>
> *Pause.*
>
> Christ! I hate all of you.
>
> *Silence.*
>
> I'm sorry, I really am sorry - I don't mean that at all. I shouldn't have said those things, sorry, sorry...

SARAH

> You shouldn't have.

Scene Two

Time has passed, it has moved into night. The lights are lowered. MAGGIE faces out front, lights low and from behind. She is back-lit. Her face is in darkness. SARAH moves outside the unit right, she makes a phone call. MIKE remains still and unconscious.

MAGGIE

> *Talking to herself.*
>
> One time, we were warm together, Mike and me.
> *Silence.*

All that time before the kids came and also when they came. When they were little he was good at getting up in the night and doing the night feed, to give me a break.

Pause.

Darling...

Pause.

It's a long time since I said that word. When did Mike last say darling to me, or sweetheart?

Pause.

How did we go cold?

Pause.

Who moved? Who...? He went somewhere, took off and shut the door and, seemed to laugh. I felt shut out. It was so gradual and we were so busy and then...

Pause.

Then the air became full of secrets. Sometimes they felt like threats and they scared me. I was scared... to ask... maybe I was afraid of what I might find out? I couldn't put a name on it, any of it, what was happening and what had changed? I banged on Mike's closed door. Who were these people I never met? I had an ache inside me and

I couldn't speak, couldn't say, my life with Mike was slithering away and, and... Then I think it began to burn me up and then, I grew cold.

Pause.

Now it is all cold.

Light on SARAH, the rest in the dark. SARAH is speaking to her brother Billy on her mobile phone.

SARAH

Billy? You got Mum's message?

Pauses for Billy's response.

Billy you should come. I know how you feel... I don't? Look whatever happened between you and Dad, he's still your dad, your father, you've only got one... You don't know that! Some people have difficulty showing love. Yes, that stuff - love... Yes, I am still with Brian, as you put it... That's not your bloody business.

MAGGIE leaves MIKE's bedside and exits.

Cut it out Billy. Look, if that is all you have to say, I'll go, but just come. You may regret it if you don't. Think - what if he doesn't make it? Yes, I do, he's as tough as old boots. No of course I didn't tell Mum I'm phoning... Come, if only for your own sake. Don't be an idiot, just come, Billy. Bye.

Silence.

Scene Three

It is still night. MIKE sits up and stretches, he swings his legs out of the bed and sits facing front.

MIKE

> *In his own voice, speaks out live to the audience. Speaks slowly.*

> To be honest with you - there's no messing if you keep your big mouth shut.

> *Pause.*

> I have.

> *Pause.*

> Blame me if you like, but for better or for worse that's what I did and I stand over my decision. It's the only way. Best way. Kept the family out of it, pure and simple. But, it has a price. Everything in this bloody world has a price. The sooner you learn that in this world the better.

Pause.

Fair play to Maggie she hung on in there. Jesus, I was mad about the woman, still am, but in this game there is no compromise, I knew it when I took it on, went in with my eyes open. She thinks I'm a shit now and who can blame her? Still, she likes the good things I've been able to give her. She bloody well does. When I get out of this little spot of bother...

Begins to lie back in the bed again.

I'll make it up to her, so I will. We'll go to the Canaries and have sex day and night again. That will put a smile on her face... and mine.

MIKE lies down as before. Silence, then low sounds of breathing, then heartbeat. THE WOMAN comes to his bedside and sits on the bed beside the unconscious MIKE.. She takes a small gun from her pocket and lets it lie in the palm of her hand.

Voice-over.

What's that for? Bit late with that aren't you?
Pause.

I haven't said anything. I'm not here. Don't know where I am, but it's great gas, girl. Really

good craic. I'm as happy as a pig in shit. And
I know about shit, but I have not met this sort
before. What's happened? Fill me in.

THE WOMAN leans over and whispers in his ear.
End of voice-over.

They took me out? The feckers! The bastards!
They didn't succeed, did they? They did? Oh they
have? Good God! I have missed the whole show.
And I gave them the slip for all these years…
What a laugh. Oh it's the luck of the draw. The
short straw this time. Can't believe it though, it
doesn't seem real somehow. But you and I knew
darling, that if we stepped in with that lot - and
we did - we knew the risk. Well, half-knew at
first and then - oh, then it was too late. There
was no going back. We knew if we made one
slip, that would be it, caput! You were a gonner.
Oh, do their methods stink! We were not working
with pussycats.

Pause.

Funny thing, I believe you could purr? If you
wanted to? Can you purr sweetheart? A kind of
sexy purr? But you and I were never lovers…
THE WOMAN gives a little laugh as she leans

forward to whisper again.

We were. Is that what you said, is that what you really said? Come back here to me this minute, woman. Come here, come here, close - closer.

THE WOMAN leans down to him again.

That's better. What did you say? We are going to be? Did I hear you say that?

Pause.

Ooooh that's nice. I like that, I really like that. I look forward to that. You're a grand girl.

Sound of heartbeat and breathing. THE WOMAN opens her black jacket and shows the red blouse.

I can see your heart, all red and blue and beating. Listen to it, listen to it. It's so loud. Are you beating the blues? Let's rock and roll baby.

He puts his hand on THE WOMAN's breasts, and she disconnects the wires that are attached to his bare chest and she lies down gently on him. They are still. Heartbeats become very loud and fast, and then become slower and slower, and softer behind MAGGIE's speech. MAGGIE comes in from the auditorium and gets up on the stage and speaks to the audience. Spot on MAGGIE.

MAGGIE

>Hello everyone. I felt I must pop back as I feel so guilty disturbing you all and interfering with the start of the play and everything; so in case you didn't understand, I had this awful news - my husband has had this terrible accident... Of course I shouldn't have kept my phone on. I thought it was off, but my guardian angel must have been flying low mustn't he? Anyway - Mike's turned the corner and I wanted you to know and everything...
>
> *THE WOMAN slips off MIKE, goes upstage behind the bed, then moves centre stage right and stands very still with her back to the action.*
>
> Must rush. Oh you see, my husband regained consciousness for a little while - when I was in the toilet - it wasn't for long but it is a good sign and the staff are much more hopeful now. But some things are so funny and make me feel everything will be alright. When Mike came round, he said please would they bring him his darling Sweetie. So the nurse came running and banging on the toilet door. They thought it was his pet name for me! But it's not. It's not his name for me at all. You'll never guess in a

hundred years whose name it is... It's his little
dog's name! The things that go though our minds
when we are out of them, if you know what I
mean. Mike loves animals, especially his young
dog. Shows the kind of man he is, underneath
everything.

*Heartbeats and breathing sounds change tempo.
SARAH enters and sits by MIKE.*

I mustn't hold you all up, and I must get back.
Thank you for being so understanding. Everyone
has been so helpful, I am grateful, thank you, I
must get back now. It is good to feel things are
on the up.

Begins to go.

Good night. Good, good night.

*MAGGIE turns back into the set and freezes.
SARAH holds MIKE's hand.*

SARAH

Dad, Dad. Do you hear me? Can you... could
you... show me something, anything, any little
sign that you hear me? We didn't hit it off, lately,
did we? I just want to say - and someone may
come and I won't be able to - so just in case I
can't say it to you later - that I have to live my

life and you live yours. I know you do, even if I
don't know how or what, because I see so little
of you now. You are never there for me, or for
Mum. You have another life and we don't know
it. Mum thinks it's another woman - I think
maybe - maybe not. I think it is something I can't
understand at all, and I think I don't want to
understand.

MIKE

On voice-over.

There's the good dog. Sit still now. You're a great
girl altogether. What would I do with out you?
You're the best girl in the world.

*MIKE slips easily out of bed. He slips his hand
from SARAH's. She does not see him get out of
bed and stays with her hand as if she was still
holding his. MIKE moves easily towards back
right where THE WOMAN comes to him. She
peels off her jacket and with her arms around his
neck they dance with their bodies close together,
ritualistically, full of tension, as when dancing
the tango. Eye to eye, they circle on one spot,
they are beautiful. They are in half-light, dim
and warm. It is a dance of death. The light on*

MIKE's bed is the same as if he was lying there but through the dance turns a more intense icy blue. SARAH continues talking to MIKE as if he was still in the bed. As far as she is concerned he is. Music is soft behind the dancing couple with heartbeat and breathing sound.

SARAH

>Listen Dad. Oh, I'm not good at this, but Dad, Dad, this is so awful - but I do care for you. I do. I have love for you, and also I do adore Brian. I know you hate it that I am with him but he is good for me - I can't explain it Dad, but he just is. Please understand - please get better Dad.
>*Whispers.*
>Get better. If you get better, I will try and give up Brian. If you talk to me. Talk to me... Talk to me, please can you? Tell me what you think, oh Dad!

MIKE and THE WOMAN continue dancing. SARAH stays at the bedside. Heartbeats and breathing sounds become fast and loud. MIKE partly collapses in THE WOMAN's arms as in a Pièta. She returns him to the bed still in their dance. She lays him on the bed, and only then does the dance end. Return to the hospital mode.

THE WOMAN takes down a white coat, puts it on, and becomes NURSE ONE again and works to revive MIKE. MAGGIE moves to MIKE's side, SARAH is stunned; then goes to the edge of the stage and dials her mobile, then returns to her father's bedside. We hear her mobile ringing and ringing, with no answer.

We hear the squeal of brakes and the bump of the crash. Sound of breathing and heartbeat stops. There is sudden and complete silence. All are still. A pause.

NURSE ONE slowly and gently disconnects MIKE from all the machines. The sounds of machines cease.

Silence.

The three women stand at his bedside. They are still.

Suddenly MIKE gets up happily and walks out front in a happy mood. He speaks live. Sunny, golden light on MIKE. He walks downstage. At the same time MAGGIE moves stage right. NURSE ONE comes to her and puts her arm around her to comfort her. MAGGIE rests

*against NURSE ONE. SARAH joins them.
Standing by and holding her mother. They face
out front. MIKE whistles a traditional Irish air.*

MAGGIE

> *Says the Rosary or just Hail Marys quietly
> behind MIKE as he sings or whistles.*
>
> Hail Mary full of grace,
>
> The Lord is with thee,
>
> Blessed art thou amongst woman,
>
> And blessed is the fruit of thy womb, Jesus

NURSE ONE

> *Continues the prayer.*
>
> Holy Mary, Mother of God
>
> Pray for us sinners,
>
> Now and at the hour of our death,
>
> Amen.
>
> *They stand still and repeat this pattern of prayer
> and response behind MIKE. MIKE sings a few
> bars of a traditional song, then whistles for his
> dog.*

MIKE

> Hey Sweetie, Hey, here girl, here.

Picks up an imaginary stick to throw.

There's a good girl. Sit. Sit. You're the best girl in the world, what would I do without you?

Mimes throwing the stick into the audience.

Go girl. Fetch. Go girl, go on, go on girl, go…
Watches as if his dog is chasing the ball out front, exits or walks onto the stage and plays with his imaginary dog happily.

Strings

A play in one act

First presented by the Druid Theatre Company in a workshop production as part of the Galway Arts Festival at the Druid Theatre, Galway, 1981, directed by Patrick Mason.

Characters

THE MUSICIAN

A woman plays:

> THE WIFE
>
> THE DAUGHTER
>
> THE MOTHER
>
> WOMAN LOVER

A man plays:

> THE HUSBAND
>
> THE FATHER
>
> THE SON
>
> MAN LOVER

Set

The action takes place in the kitchen of a holiday home in the west of Ireland.

Bare stage. Upstage a kitchen sink, stainless steel, free-standing, supported by plain wooden legs. To right of sink an apron, natural linen, hangs on a hook. To centre right stage is a plain kitchen table with two chairs, all in natural wood. These objects are good quality modern furniture. A chair is left downstage on the floor. Beside this chair lies a newspaper, an unopened packet of cigarettes and a book.

Scene One

THE MUSICIAN sits downstage left and sets the mood and the change of mood and place from one scene to the next through the choice and tone of music. THE MUSICIAN plays jaunty pop or folk music. Sounds of conversation over a dinner table off stage, perhaps singing along to the music.

Music continues while THE WIFE enters from left, crosses to apron and takes it down, stands with back to audience in front of sink and ties the apron strings behind her back. She begins washing up.

THE HUSBAND enters, goes to the chair downstage left, and sits. He is smoking a small cigar. He relaxes.

Music continues and develops a harsher tone and ends on a note of discord. Silence.

> *THE WIFE sniffs.*

THE HUSBAND

> Don't sniff.
>
> *Pause.*

THE WIFE

> I'm not sniffing.

THE HUSBAND

> You were sniffing. I've got ears haven't I?
>
> *Pause.*
>
> *THE WIFE sniffs.*
>
> Did you fetch the paper?

THE WIFE

> I did.

THE HUSBAND

> And my cigarettes?

THE WIFE

> Yes.

THE HUSBAND

> Where are they?

THE WIFE

> Haven't you got eyes? There, beside you.

THE HUSBAND

> Keep your hair on.
>
> *Picks up the paper and reads. THE WIFE sniffs.*
>
> Would you ever stop that damn sniffing?

THE WIFE

> *Keeping back to audience.*
>
> For God's sake can't you see? All I do here is

exchange this sink for the one at home. Let's get away, you say. A weekend in the west would do us good, you say. Ha ha. Who does the preparing? The food? The clothes? Organising the kids? Me, me. You in there just chat and laugh...

THE HUSBAND

Hey, stop that. I don't mind the washing up. That's no problem, I'll do the bloody washing up. Why can't you ask like a civilised person instead of making this damn fuss over nothing? It's not worth crying over...

THE WIFE

Furious and weeping.

You fool. You bloody silly fool. That's no good. Doing the washing up like some fecking martyr. It's not like that, it's just...

They are face to face and glaring. Glaring like fighting cocks. Silence. They are still.

Scene Two

THE MUSICIAN plays gentle, soft music. THE WIFE unties the apron strings, takes apron off and hangs it up. She now becomes THE DAUGHTER and moves downstage to sit on the floor beside THE HUSBAND who now becomes THE FATHER. He picks up the book and reads to her. Music continues behind the monologue.

THE DAUGHTER

> I liked the smell of your jacket, Dad, when I sat on your knee when I was little and you read stories to me, the stories your mother read to you, Alice in Wonderland and the scary Water Babies. You always read in a special sing-song sort of voice and sometimes, when Mum was there, this would make her smile. I knew she found it funny and I'd try not to giggle too because you would stop reading and sigh. You looked so offended. And I liked sitting on your knee being read to, even if your watch chain did stick into my ribs a bit.
>
> *Pause.*
>
> I liked it when you stroked my arm. Sometimes

you read the Fairy Queen.

Silence. They are still.

Scene Three

THE MUSICIAN plays discordant chords. THE DAUGHTER goes and takes down the apron and returns to stand at the sink as THE WIFE, back to the audience, tying the strings behind her back as before. She sniffs.

THE HUSBAND

>*Getting up and going towards her, shouting.*
>
>For Christ's sake woman. I offer help and you throw it at me. I can't do anything any more. I can't do anything.

THE WIFE

>When did you last try?

THE HUSBAND

>If you don't want me here I'll go back to the others. I only came in to help, to keep you company. You're always complaining you're lonely, that we never get away.

THE WIFE

> *Turning.*
>
> How good of you to keep your dear wife company. Cheer up the little woman. Jolly her along. Thank you so much. I'm so grateful.

THE HUSBAND

> Bloody stupid bitch.
>
> *He begins to leave.*
>
> I don't know why I bother.
>
> *They are still.*
>
> *Silence.*

Scene Four

THE MUSICIAN plays cocktail party music. THE WIFE takes off apron and hangs it up as before, becomes THE DAUGHTER. THE FATHER and THE DAUGHTER take a wine glass each and mingle with imaginary guests at the cocktail party. THE FATHER is talking to other guests and THE DAUGHTER is looking towards him and sipping her drink.

THE FATHER

> *Talking to guests.*
>
> Last weekend, a great breeze, you're right. It blew like mad on Sunday. Didn't take the reefs out the whole weekend. Marvellous sail, she went like a bird. Old Billy wouldn't go out at all. You know him. He hugged the bar.
>
> *Laughing.*

THE DAUGHTER

> Going to those cocktail parties with you and Mum, I stood around amongst your friends, sipping sherry, which I hated. Your friends would ask me, 'What are you going to do when you leave school?' I said, 'Become a painter.'

THE FATHER

> Oh yes, my daughter, she has grown up. She's going to art school...

THE DAUGHTER

> Their reaction was always the same. I could see it in their minds, wishy-washy water colours, bowls of limp anemones. A nice thing for a girl to do.
>
> *Pause.*

Before marriage. Fill in the time.

THE FATHER

She has quite a little talent…

THE DAUGHTER

Then they'd say 'You don't like that dreadful modern stuff do you? You know that chap, whatshisname? Picasso? A child could do that. You know, even I could do stuff like that. Ha ha.' When I said, 'Yes, I do like Picasso's work,' they talked about something else.

THE FATHER is joking and laughing with other guests.

I hated the way, Dad, you were taken in by stupid women.

Pause.

When they were pretty. You were very gullible, and when they flattered you, you beamed and glowed. I suppose I must have been jealous but I didn't know it. You would say…

THE FATHER

All women are wonderful…

THE DAUGHTER

I hated that.

They are still. Silence.

Scene Five

THE MUSICIAN plays cheerful pop music. THE DAUGHTER now becomes THE MOTHER, THE FATHER becomes THE SON.

THE MOTHER

> *Calling.*
>
> Are you alright, dear?
>
> *Listens.*
>
> Would you like another cup of tea, dear?

THE SON

> *From off stage.*
>
> No thanks, Mum.

THE MOTHER

> I've ironed your shirt, it's on your bed, dear.
>
> *Pause.*
>
> John rang dear, said he'd ring back, dear.
> Something about the car, dear.

THE SON

> *Entering.*

Did you pick up that part for me from Westbrooks?

THE MOTHER

Yes, I did, dear. I put it in the study, dear.

THE SON

OK, Mother. I'm off. I'm eating at the Greek restaurant tonight. John says it's worth a try. Don't wait up, though I don't expect to be late.

THE MOTHER

All right, dear.

Pause.

Will you leave at nine tomorrow, dear?

THE SON

Yes, I need to leave by nine at the latest.

THE MOTHER

I'll give you a call then. I'll give you a call about eight.

THE SON

OK, Mother. See you, 'night.

Exits.

THE MOTHER

Pause.

'Night, 'night, dear.

Silence.

Scene Six

THE MUSICIAN plays strident music gradually becoming more gentle. THE MOTHER now becomes THE WIFE, THE SON becomes THE HUSBAND. THE WIFE stands at the sink. THE HUSBAND, sits down. He is irritated.

THE HUSBAND

> I don't see the point of coming down for the weekend if we're going to fight all the time. We could do that just as well at home.
>
> *Pause.*
>
> What's happening to us? We used to be able to communicate?

THE WIFE

> *She turns towards him.*
>
> Oh, yes we did.
>
> We shared.
>
> *Both come down centre stage and sit on the floor.*

THE HUSBAND is with THE WIFE during the final stages of labour, she is bearing down..

THE MUSICIAN drums heartbeats.

THE HUSBAND

    That was great love. Rapid breathing now. Pant.

THE WIFE

    Pants.

    Oh my God. How am I doing? Is the head showing?

THE HUSBAND

    Yes. Yes it is. Black hair.

    Excited.

    It's got black hair. You're doing fine. Just great. Won't be many more pushes.

THE WIFE

    It's coming again now. Here it is again.

    She holds her breath and pushes down hard. She ends with an explosion of breath.

    That was a big one…

    Rests back on THE HUSBAND panting.

THE HUSBAND

    My God, you're wonderful. You're doing great.

We're nearly there love. Only a few more pushes.

THE WIFE

Here we go again.

Another strong push.

THE HUSBAND

Don't push now. Pant, pant. The head's coming.

They're saying don't push.

She pants.

Well done. Great.

Hold it. Hold it. It's coming.

The baby's head is born.

There you are.

THE WIFE is looking down at the baby's head. She pants, drawing breath and resting between the contractions.

Another push for the shoulders love. You've nearly made it, nearly there.

THE WIFE

Oh my God, here's another. Here goes... Fuck. Christ Almighty...

THE HUSBAND

Keep pushing. A big one. For the shoulders. Push.

Down the back... Push.

With extreme effort THE WIFE pushes with all her might, eyes shut.

Hold it love. Don't push now. Don't push. Hold it. Hold it.

THE WIFE pants hard and rapidly, then with her hands between her legs she mimes helping the baby to be born.

THE WIFE

Oh you're here! You're a girl.

THE MUSICIAN stops heartbeat.

THE WIFE brings the baby up gently over her stomach to lie on her belly, its head between her breasts. She is exhausted and exalted.

Oh she's so funny. So wet and little, and funny.

Silence. She is holding her child to her as they both gaze at her.

THE HUSBAND

Hello little funny face.

THE WIFE

She's beautiful.

Pause.

Isn't she beautiful?

THE WIFE rests in THE HUSBAND's arms as they look at their newborn child. They are still. Silence. Back to the present.

Very gently.

We were close then.

Pause.

THE HUSBAND

Yes.

THE WIFE

Closer than making love.

THE HUSBAND

Closer

Silence.

I was scared of the birth, but I didn't tell you. I think you knew. Mother didn't like the idea of my going. No place for a man, was the way she thought. None of that sort of thing in her day. Then I thought, hell, why should you do it all on your own? It's my child too.

Pause.

I've always been afraid of blood, it makes me feel sick. Then faint. I hated myself for that.

Pause.

I never knew it was such hard work for a woman to have a baby.

Silence.

THE WIFE

I'm glad you came in the end. I needed you. Being pregnant is a bit like getting on a bus you can't get off. You have to go on to the terminus. However much you are told, you don't know what is coming. Nobody but you can do it. You're alone.

Pause.

I remember lying here in the first stages of labour and the nurse coming and putting out the baby clothes, tucking in the aired blanket in the empty cot and I thought, how stupid she is, who's having a baby? Then I realised it was me!

Pause.

And I felt bad as I thought I was letting everyone down not getting on with it quickly enough.

Silence. THE WIFE and THE HUSBAND remain still.

THE MUSICIAN plays, perhaps only a few harsh discords.

THE WIFE returns to the sink putting on the apron, tying the strings behind her back as before. THE HUSBAND sits in chair left as before.

THE WIFE sniffs.

THE HUSBAND

> Don't sniff.
>
> *Silence.*
>
> We're just like a long playing record...

THE WIFE

> Just why do we do this...?

THE HUSBAND

> Switch a switch and we turn on a row.
>
> *Sings.*
>
> Some dis-enchanted evening.

THE WIFE

> Why do we let it happen?

THE HUSBAND

> We're very experienced.

THE WIFE

> *Turns.*
>
> You never miss a cue...

THE HUSBAND

>You're very good at it. I think you really enjoy it.

THE WIFE

>You're quite professional yourself.
>
>*Silence.*
>
>*THE WIFE sniffs.*
>
>*THE HUSBAND leaps from the chair in irritation and walks to THE WIFE and thrusts a hankie at her.*

THE HUSBAND

>Here, use this.

THE WIFE

>*Furious.*
>
>You shit.
>
>*They are face to face. Still.*

Scene Seven

THE MUSICIAN plays music for happy lovers. MAN LOVER, formerly THE HUSBAND, sits in chair facing right, he reads a book. He is waiting for WOMAN LOVER in a hotel. THE WIFE takes off apron, hangs it up and sits in chair, facing front right as WOMAN LOVER.

MAN LOVER

> Remember the first time...?

WOMAN LOVER

> The first time together...

MAN LOVER

> That hotel.

WOMAN LOVER

> The odd little woman receptionist, she had a moustache! I got a lift to get to you. Friends were driving to the country. I sat in the car. They were all ordinary. I felt extraordinary. I tried to be just me, but I was all high and...

MAN LOVER

> Your voice on the phone sounded squeaky. For a weekend you said. Could I find a hotel, not too expensive.
>
> *Pause.*
>
> I looked in the paper. The Hermitage or the Angler's Return, what a choice.

WOMAN LOVER

> We stayed at The Hermitage.

MAN LOVER

> Funny sort of hermits.

WOMAN LOVER

> They thought I was spending the weekend at my sister's. Her fourth was due in a week.

MAN LOVER

> I was able to get the neighbours to step in and feed the animals. They're easy about it as I ask so seldom.

WOMAN LOVER

> My friends dropped me at a bus stop. They had white faces like puppets as they waved me goodbye. My knees wobbled as I went upstairs and then…
>
> *Turns.*
>
> You were there.
>
> *MAN LOVER rises and they hold each other.*
>
> Did you feel the panic in me as you held me close? I felt like a traitor. A voice inside me said no, you can't do this. You can't. But you kept holding me, and then…
>
> *Pause.*
>
> I became calm. Close.

Using the table on its side as a headboard, WOMAN LOVER and HER LOVER sit side-by-side as if in a double-bed.

And oh the room, the terrible wallpaper...

MAN LOVER

Mauve and yellow.

WOMAN LOVER

And how we wrapped my knickers around the light over the bed because it glared...

MAN LOVER

And burned a hole in them.

WOMAN LOVER

Oh we drank brandy because we'd got frozen climbing the cliffs, and we sang, and jumped up and down on the bed and your head just missed the light in the ceiling.

They are laughing.

...so we huddled under the bedclothes and giggled until I felt sick and you... stroked my arm and said...

MAN LOVER

I never knew you had so many freckles.

Silence. They are still.

THE MUSICIAN plays quiet and sad music.

They move and sit opposite each other at the table and drink coffee. No eye contact.

I don't say what I want to say. So we sit here. Happy? Yes, yes. We are happy for these few moments. This short time we spend together.

Silence.

She knows I can't say it. That I can't say 'Come, I'm here.' Perhaps I should say it. Force the issue. But I don't.

Pause.

I know what she would say anyway, 'the children...' Or do I know?

Silence

I would hate to be someone who destroys, breaks things up. It seems important that everything should grow. There's enough death.

Pause.

She's so full of energy. And the kids, they're great kids. I wouldn't, couldn't, harm any of that. She'd never dream of it anyway. I know she wouldn't. She's...

Pause.

She's in some odd way I don't understand... Who can understand these messes? Love should be so simple, why isn't it simple? It's been going on for centuries, should have got the hang of it by now for Christ's sake. It's such a straightforward small word. Love. What is fucking love? How do we give it to anyone? Who gave us the big idea it's easy, when it's not? It's difficult. Bloody difficult.

They are still and silent.

WOMAN LOVER

This is the only peace I know. When he calls. We can talk and talk, that's always easy. I can say anything to him. It is so good when we can be together. Relaxed. Simple. I never believed I could share so much with someone. And we laugh. It's good to laugh.

Pause

He never mentions anything, but I can see him thinking. He's asking all the same. Sometimes I want to scream.

They are still. Silence.

Scene Eight

THE MUSICIAN plays the original music from scene one ending with harsh discordant chords. Both THE HUSBAND and THE WIFE return to positions that they took at the beginning of the play. THE WIFE returns to the sink and puts on apron in the same way, tying the strings behind her back. THE HUSBAND sits in the same position as at the start of the play.

THE HUSBAND
>Don't sniff.

THE WIFE
>I'm not sniffing.

THE HUSBAND
>You were. I've got ears. Did you fetch the paper?

THE WIFE
>Yes.

THE HUSBAND
>And my cigarettes?

THE WIFE
>I did.

THE HUSBAND

>Where are they?

THE WIFE

>Don't you ever look? They are there, beside you.

THE HUSBAND

>Keep your hair on.
>
>*THE WIFE sniffs.*
>
>Stop that damn sniffing, you're driving me mad...

THE WIFE

>*Explodes.*
>
>For God's sake. CAN'T YOU SEE...!
>
>*They are still.*
>
>*Silence.*
>
>*THE WIFE takes off the apron and hangs it up. She returns to the sink with her back to the audience. Lights fade, leaving light on the apron only. Light on apron fades to blackout.*

Cake

A mime/play

Note

I visualise the stage with three free-standing doors. But that poses difficulties, as doors often do, (doors sway and wobble and do not ever slam on stage) and may be difficult to construct. Possibly one could use a door frame only, which could be made strong and firm or one could indicate the door by lighting or a chalk drawing on the floor.

Another solution is to indicate the door by sound or an actor could open the mime/play, by coming on stage and drawing the three openings on the floor: turning the imaginary handles, opening these doors one by one, with sound track of door opening, and then slamming (very loudly) thus setting up the scene. Then exit. The audience at that stage, are well informed of the set.

Characters

THE ACTOR *a man or a woman*

VOICES *live or recorded*

Set

Staged in the round with the audience very close. In a room, not a theatre as such.

Three doors, spaced apart, no wall in between. Centre stage and forward from the doors is one small square table on which lies a white plate. This plate is nearly the size of the table. Beside the white plate lies a large knife.

Scene One

Empty stage. Lights up.

Silence.

Sounds of sea. Loud sound of someone eating. Loud sound of someone swallowing. Eating/ swallowing continues.

Silence.

Sound of someone walking quickly up stone steps. Stops in mid-step.

Silence.

All three doors burst open.

Silence.

VOICES: Sudden sound of a crowd bursting into the room.

THE ACTOR gets up from a seat in the audience to welcome the guests. These invisible guests push him, shake his hand, jostle, laugh, push presents on him. He is almost submerged by this as if a great tide has swept in on him. VOICES become the sound of the sea, then back to VOICES. THE ACTOR is swept towards the square table. He is shy. VOICES sometimes intelligible and sometimes not.

THE ACTOR is going to have to cut the cake. Some imaginary people are in the way. He has to push through them to the table. At last he stands behind the table.

Sudden silence.

THE ACTOR stands still and looks at the plate. White spotlight on plate. THE ACTOR leans over. Takes a deep breath. Loud sound of blowing. Lights out.

Silence.

VOICES giggle.

Silence.

One thin quivery VOICE starts singing, with giggles interspersed throughout.

VOICE

Happy birthday to...

Stops.

Happy b...

Stops.

Happy...

Stops.

Hap...

Stops.

Ha...

Stops.

Ha... Ha... Ha... Ha...

End of giggles.

Lights on full.

Loudly, VOICES sing Happy Birthday omitting the word 'you' and interspersing traditional lines with:

You look like a monkey and smell like one... *omitting the word 'too.'*

THE ACTOR cuts the cake and hands slices to his guests.

VOICES make crowd noises and these become loud. Stop. Guzzling. Loud guzzling.

Silence.

All doors shut.

THE ACTOR stands still by the table and replaces the knife across the plate.

Silence.

Returns to his seat in the audience.

Spot on white plate and knife. Lights fade leaving only spot on plate.

Lights out sharply.

VOICES giggle.

www.ingramcontent.com/pod-product-compliance
Lightning Source LLC
Chambersburg PA
CBHW070550300426
44113CB00011B/1848